# Preparing the Liturgical Year 2:

## LENT – EASTER AND
## ADVENT – CHRISTMAS

*Corbin Eddy*

NOVALIS

THE LITURGICAL PRESS

Design: Eye-to-Eye Design, Toronto

Layout: Suzanne Latourelle

Illustrations: Eugene Kral

Series Editor: Bernadette Gasslein

© 1997, Novalis, Saint Paul University, Ottawa, Ontario, Canada

Business Office: Novalis, 49 Front Street East, 2nd floor, Toronto, Ontario M5E 1B3

Published in the United States of America by The Liturgical Press, Box 7500, Collegeville, MN 56321-7500

Novalis: ISBN 2 89088 890-8

Liturgical Press: ISBN 0-8146-2488-X
A Liturgical Press Book.
Library of Congress data available on request.

Excerpts from the English translations of: *The Roman Missal* ©1973 International Committee on English in the Liturgy, Inc Used by permission. All rights reserved.

Printed in Canada.

Canadian Cataloguing in Publication

Eddy, Corbin, 1942-
    Preparing the liturgical year
(Preparing for liturgy)
Contents: 1. Sunday and the Paschal Triduum
    2. Lent-East and Advent-Christmas
ISBN 2089088-793-6 (v.1) -
ISBN 2-89088-890-8 (v.2)
    1. Church year. 2. Catholic Church—Liturgy.
I. Title. II. Series.
BX 1970.E33 1997          264'.02   C97-900373-3

# Contents

# Introduction

This book, like Volume 1, is designed to help communities review their basic patterns of common worship so that these patterns may be as effective as possible in renewing the church's sense of common history, identity and mission. The sequence of the books and their chapters is designed to help you establish some priorities. After looking at the paschal mystery, we look at the two principal celebrations of the year: Sunday and the paschal Triduum (volume 1). Only in light of these central considerations do we move to reflect on the liturgical seasons. So, please be sure to read volume 1!

## *Guiding Principles: A Summary*

1. Think prepare rather than plan. The strength of ritual-liturgical celebration lies in its stable format which links it to the prayer of the whole church.

2. The task of preparing the liturgical year involves the ongoing education and formation of the assembly, the particular servant ministries and ordained ministers—deacon, presbyter, and bishop.

3. Liturgy is a ritual event in the life of the church. Preparing the liturgical year requires a deep respect and reverence for the people of a particular community.

4. The lectionary and sacramentary with their pastoral notes, the *General Norms for the Liturgical Year and Calendar*, along with the liturgical calendar (ordo) prepared by the Canadian Conference of Catholic Bishops, provide basic resources about the seasons, reflect the tradition, present many options and much flexibility.

5. Those preparing the liturgy will need to review the many options provided in the official books so that choices make a genuine contribution to the assembly's experience of a particular celebration.

# CHAPTER 1

# Lent

Only in the light of the great triduum can the Lenten period, which leads up to it and the Easter season which flows from it, best be lived and understood.

Although the church has always observed Lent in a conscious and deliberate way, many people still experience it as a time of personal spiritual effort to grow in discipline and will power. They undertake disciplined prayer, fasting and almsgiving as a kind of personal workout with little conscious connection to the mystery of baptismal renewal. The sackcloth and ashes of Ash Wednesday become stark reminders of death and the need to prepare for God's judgment rather than acknowledgments of our infidelity to the dignity proclaimed in the white garment and chrism of Easter baptism.

## Lent: Baptism and Conversion

This shift from an emphasis on a living community of faith rooted in baptism to personal asceticism for the sake of the soul's salvation or as preparation for death and judgment arises from several factors. The separation of Christian initiation from the triduum, the absence of adult catechumens as a visible focus for Lenten preparation, and the church's subsequent lack of experience in self-renewal by receiving new members and reconciling penitents all have contributed to this imbalance. The *Constitution on the Sacred Liturgy* (nos. 109-110) is very clear on these points:

> *Lent is marked by two themes, the baptismal and the penitential. By recalling or preparing for baptism and by repentance, this season disposes the faithful, as they more diligently listen to the word of God and devote themselves to prayer, to celebrate the paschal mystery. The baptismal and penitential aspects of Lent are to be given greater prominence in both the liturgy and liturgical catechesis. Hence:*

*a. More use is to be made of the baptismal features proper to the lenten liturgy; some of those from an earlier era are to be restored as may seem advisable.*

*b. The same is to apply to the penitential elements. As regards catechesis, it is important to impress on the minds of the faithful not only the social consequences of sin but also the essence of the virtue of penance, namely, detestation of sin as an offense against God; the role of the church in penitential practices is not to be neglected and the people are to be exhorted to pray for sinners.*

*During Lent, penance should be not only inward and individual, but also outward and social. The practice of penance should be fostered, however, in ways that are possible in our own times and in different regions and according to the circumstances of the faithful.*

The conciliar text highlights two dominant emphases: baptism and conversion. We will need to stress these themes repeatedly as the church renews its understanding of the season. Lent is the time of immediate preparation for the sacraments of initiation (including confirmation and first eucharist for the young people of the parish and their families), and a time of baptismal recommitment for the rest of the parish. In this light it is easy to see how the sacrament of reconciliation will be a major feature in the Lenten observance of many who take seriously the call to deeper and renewed conversion.

Christians relate the forty days of Lent to the biblical number 40, a reference to times of intense preparation and prayer: Israel's forty years in the desert; Christ's forty-day fast. Most people have learned to calculate these forty days beginning with Ash Wednesday and counting up to Holy Saturday. This makes forty-six days, minus six Sundays, for a total of forty fast days. An older, more traditional calculation counts from the First Sunday of Lent to the beginning of the triduum.

## The Three Periods of Lent

When we understand that Lent leads to the triduum and prepares for initiation or reconciliation, we can distinguish three periods. This breakdown helps develop an approach to preparing the season.

1. Announcement: On Ash Wednesday, the faithful are called to fasting and penance with the traditional symbols of penitence, sackcloth and ashes. The text from Joel sounds a trumpet call to change of heart and reconciliation. In ancient times this led to the public celebration of reconciliation on the morning of the Thursday of Holy Week, the last day of Lent at which time the sackcloth and ashes were put aside.

The three days following Ash Wednesday summarize the agenda to be considered and lived out in preparation for reconciliation and renewal of baptismal vows at Easter.

2. Period of purification and enlightenment: The First Sunday of Lent, which emphasizes Jesus' temptations, stands as the real beginning day of Lent with the rite of election. In light of Jesus' temptations, catechumens are called to a final, intense period of openness to Christ's own Spirit who, with their cooperation, purifies and enlightens them for life and mission. The scrutinies, celebrated on the Third, Fourth and Fifth Sundays of Lent increase the intensity of this movement. (For more information on this topic, please see *Preparing the Rites of Initiation* in this series).

3. Immediate preparation for the triduum: From the Fifth Sunday of Lent on, the scriptures focus on the passion of Christ. His struggles as his own passion-passover approaches powerfully summarize the nature and consequences of the Christian commitment to be celebrated during the triduum.

## *The Mystery Unfolded in the Lectionary*

As throughout the liturgical year, the lectionary for Lent functions on a three-year cycle that reflects the two-fold character of Lent I described earlier in this chapter.

Year A, which may be used in any year when there are adult candidates for Christian initiation, highlights the inner meaning of baptism. Years B and C emphasize repentance and penance. These foci are especially evident on the third, fourth and fifth

Sundays. Even in this context, it is still possible to chart the Sunday gospel and to highlight certain aspects of the paschal mystery. This should help those responsible for preparing liturgy to use their imagination and experience to create a kind of lens through which they can view and celebrate the mystery on a particular occasion.

The chart on the next page will help you see the season, with its component parts, as a whole, and view it with a clear sense of direction.

## *Recontextualizing Traditional Practices*

The traditional practices of Lent—prayer, fasting and almsgiving—are best re-contextualized in this overall spirit. They express the dynamic tension in genuine baptismal faith, which is at the same time both personal and communal-social, expressed in internal and external ways, and directed to a sacramental-mystical communion with the death and rising of Christ.

During Lent, prayer involves personal introspection and reordering of priorities in light of the gospel. It likewise involves coming together as a community in celebrations of the word and sacrament which contextualize this personal experience in the community's life and the church's ancient tradition. The intensity of individual journeys and the breadth of the common tradition enrich and challenge each other.

The imposition of ashes and the sacrament of reconciliation bring together both the individual call to conversion and reconciliation with God, and the invitation to all humanity to engage in this experience as members of one body. Each person experiences the imposition of ashes in a unique way, and, in this same gesture, expresses communion with the whole church over the ages. The sacrament of reconciliation climaxes this personal journey towards forgiveness and reconciliation and celebrates, at the same time, the whole people's reconciliation with God who draws all into deeper communion in the death and rising of Christ.

| Sunday | Scripture Yr. A | Scripture Yr. B | Scripture Yr. C | Images and Aspects of the Paschal Mystery; invitations to dying and rising |
|---|---|---|---|---|
| First Sunday of Lent | Matthew 4:1-11 Jesus fasted forty days and was put to the test. | Mark 1: 12-14 Jesus was tempted by Satan, and the angels waited on him | Luke 4: 1-13 The spirit led Jesus into the wilderness where he was tempted. | Desert: wild beasts. Struggle with sin and evil. Nourished by the word of God. Ultimate dependence on God. Struggle points to the cross. |
| Second Sunday of Lent | Matthew 17:1-9 Jesus' face shone like the sun. | Mark 9:2-10 This is my son, the beloved Listen to him. | Luke 9: 28b-36 While Jesus prayed, the appearance of his face changed. | Light; Experience of prayer; Moses and Elijah: their stories point to the nature of Jesus' person, role and mission. Moving on from the "mountain top" experience. Transfiguration pointing to resurrection. |
| Third Sunday of Lent | John 4: 5-42 The water that I will give will become a spring of water gushing up to eternal life | John 2: 13-25 Destroy this temple and in three days will raise I it up. | Luke 13:1-9 Unless you turn back to God, you will perish as they did. | A: Thirst; the wells to which we go for life; water of life, living water; inner spring. B-C: The temple; Integrity of worship; Limitations of religious institutions; Interpreting God's will-a dangerous game; Conversion as a change of mind, a new way of thinking; Mystery of chance evil, mystery of human cruelty. |
| Fourth Sunday of Lent | John 9:1-41 The man who was blind washed his eyes, and returned, able to see. | John 3: 14-21 God so loved the world that he gave his only Son, the we may have eternal life | Luke 15: 1-3. 11-32 This brother of yours was dead and has come to life. | A: sight-eyes opened; enlightenment; pool of water; B-C: Serpent raised in the desert; God's love of the world; Loving darkness, fearing light; coming home as reconciliation-coming back to life. Father running in welcome. |
| Fifth Sunday of Lent | John 11:1-45 I am the resurrection and the life. | John 12:20-33 If a grain of wheat falls into the earth and dies, it bears much fruit. | John 8: 1-11 Let anyone among you who is without sin be the first to throw a stone. | A: grave; rock, corruption and renewal; being bound and being set free; B-C: fruitfulness of life coming out of death; human solidarity in sinfulness and need of mercy; futility of passing judgment. |

Fasting can have the same dynamic. It empties a person and can even bring about a level of consciousness—and experience—quite different from that of being "full"—"fat and happy." It requires personal effort and discipline resulting from personal acts and choices. Likewise it can provide an experience of communion with the world's material and spiritual hungers. When undertaken in solidarity with a community of faith, it can be a deeply religious experience.

When united with prayer and fasting as the third component of a penitential spirit, almsgiving also expresses ongoing renewal and conversion. Believers review, analyse and make concrete decisions about their relationship to material things in light of the condition of the planet, the needs of society, and the needs and aspirations of the poor in the community. Community resources are often pooled during Lent in food banks, third world development initiatives, and other community concerns.

## *Lenten Solidarity*

If Lent is about baptism and conversion, it will be important for the whole assembly to become as fully involved as possible with all those preparing for the sacraments of initiation. Journeying with them provides a living context for ongoing conversion and rededication to an ever-deepening communion with the death and resurrection of Christ. A communal celebration of the sacrament of reconciliation will take a central place in the season, ideally in the spirit of the scrutinies celebrated with those preparing for baptism.

Materials that reflect these Lenten emphases can be used at home and at all parish meetings. Together with catechesis on fasting and opportunities for almsgiving, they will strengthen the community's solidarity in its Lenten observance. Parish leaders will want to study the many resources available and make careful choices.

The liturgies, with their powerful series of biblical texts—especially on Sundays, can take on a sober, intense flavour that leads the assembly into the spirit of Easter renewal.

## A Liturgical Spirituality

These considerations work together in a cumulative way to form a liturgical, baptismal spirituality within the assembly. This spirituality gathers and organizes all aspects of Christian religious experience and practice around what is truly central: the death and resurrection of Christ into which believers are invited and immersed through the liturgy. Its core is the sacraments of initiation: baptism-confirmation-eucharist. Chapter One, Section I of Vatican II's *Constitution on the Liturgy* is well worth re-reading in this light.

## The Initiation of Children and Young People

This perspective offers us the best understanding and appreciation of the Christian initiation of children and young people. Central to their catechesis and preparation for the sacraments will be a full experience of the season of Lent. This provides for them, as for the adult elect, the basis for ongoing renewal which will develop and mature as they experience Lent again and again, and grow in "wisdom, age and grace" (Luke 2: 52). Imagine the difference between a celebration of the first communion of children on Easter Sunday morning (white garments, baptismal candles and all), and a "quasi-private" celebration at two o'clock in the afternoon on Mothers' Day. Perhaps the contrast is too sharp, the "Easter ideal" not possible in all communities, but it serves to illustrate the main issues.

## First Reconciliation

First reconciliation for children can also be incorporated and contextualized within the community's experience of Ash Wednesday's enrolment liturgy and the subsequent celebration of Lenten reconciliation. A family celebration of the sacrament in the early evening during the last week of Lent, for example, could include the first celebration of reconciliation for children. It would solidify the community, and incorporate children into its ritual life. It would contribute in an important way to the process of initiating them into the tradition, life and practice of the whole church.

## Nature Passes from Death to Life

The lengthening of days and approaching spring in the northern hemisphere where the liturgical year took its shape make their wordless contribution to the passage from death to life celebrated in the paschal mystery. The title by which this time is popularly known, "Lent," is actually derived from the Anglo-Saxon word meaning "spring." The great christological hymns found, for example, in Ephesians 3 and Colossians 1 along with the last chapter of the Book of Revelation have dramatic universal-cosmic overtones. They relate the mystery of the risen Christ to the destiny of the whole universe, and the ongoing call to the restoration and renewal of the earth and its resources. This largely neglected aspect of the Lent-Easter experience needs more emphasis in our own social and cultural context.

## Catechesis

Catechesis for those involved in preparing the liturgy as well as for the community in general will be most fruitful if it is founded on the basics outlined in this chapter:

• the centrality of the initiation sacraments to the celebration of the paschal mystery which comes to a climax in the liturgical celebrations of this seasons;

• renewed conversion celebrated in the sacrament of reconciliation for those already initiated which leads to baptismal renewal at Easter;

• the experience of prayer, fasting, and almsgiving interpreted in this overall context;

• the way in which the lectionary provides a framework for meditating on and living out this central experience of faith.

## Priorities

In addition to these elements of catechesis, the principal goals and concerns of all responsible for liturgical preparation will be to facilitate drawing people into this core experience of the Christian faith. Key to effective liturgical preparation, especially during this season of initiation, is the conviction that liturgy's repetitive ritual patterns deepen the full, conscious and active participation of the assembly. In a complex, hectic, social and cultural environment, the liturgy will be most fruitful if it truly centres on these basic elements in a consciously disciplined way. Innovations or the development of annual "themes," etc. distract from the essential core. Avoid them!

## *In Summary*

The *Constitution on the Liturgy*, 109-110, summarizes the core content and spirit of the season:

1. Two themes, the baptismal and the penitential, mark Lent.

2. Give the baptismal and penitential aspects of Lent greater prominence in both the liturgy and liturgical catechesis.

3. Catechesis needs to impress on the minds of the faithful not only the social consequences of sin but also the essence of the virtue of penance.

4. During Lent, penance should be both inward and individual, and outward and social. Its practice should be fostered in ways that are possible in our own communities.

## *Discussion Questions*

1. How, in our parish, do we currently express the baptismal spirituality so central to Lent? What could enhance and better express this in our celebrations?

2. How do we accompany adults and young people preparing for the sacraments of initiation during these final days of preparation? How does this accompaniment enhance our own baptismal renewal?

3. How do we express and live the public penitential dimension of Lent? What balance have we achieved between this aspect and the baptismal dimension of Lent? How might we achieve a better balance?

4. How do we encourage the process and celebration of reconciliation during Lent? How do we accompany young people who are celebrating first reconciliation?

5. What are we doing to encourage and deepen the traditions of prayer, fasting and almsgiving in harmony with the liturgy? Check out lectionary study, faith sharing, devotional materials prepared for use in the home.

6. Do we build from year to year on the tone, style and environment of the season through music, posture, movement? How do we make Lent feel different from Ordinary Time?

CHAPTER 2

# The Easter Season

In joy and thanksgiving the church celebrates the unfolding mystery of Christ's resurrection during the Easter season. It flows out of the triduum (see volume 1), beginning on the evening of Easter Sunday and concluding on the fiftieth day of Easter, Pentecost Sunday. Easter's fifty days celebrate in a single festival a "week of weeks"; as a season it is sometimes called the "Great Sunday."

The *General Norms for the Liturgical Year and the Calendar* promulgated by Paul VI in 1969 established the restoration of the unity of this fifty-day period as a priority. Paragraph 22 insists that "the fifty days from Easter to Pentecost are celebrated as one feast," and the document goes on to point out that the "singing of the alleluia is characteristic of these days."

The seven weeks between Easter and Pentecost are above all other seasons of the year the time of Christian joy: the joy of knowing that the Lord Jesus is victorious over the forces of sin and evil, even over death, and is risen to everlasting life. There is the joy of sharing in his resurrection through baptism, and of sharing the eucharist now in anticipation of the feast of the world to come. There is the joy of living as citizens of a world redeemed and restored in a new springtime of hope, our hearts lifted up in Christ.

Two great feasts, Ascension and Pentecost, bring the season to a close. Ascension is not a separate feast, but a celebration of Christ's way of being present now to the church. The "right hand of the Father" suggests Christ's exercise of eternal authority. From this position he communicates his Spirit to the church, his risen body at work in the world.

Similarly, Pentecost is not a separate feast, but the grand finale of Easter's fifty days. During "great Sunday" we have focused on the risen Christ sending the Spirit, for the whole season celebrates in an integrated way the mystery of the church, which continues to arise out of the reality of Christ's death and resurrection. We read the Acts of the Apostles in this light during the Easter Season rather than after Pentecost, where it would seem to fit chronologically, because Pentecost solemnly concludes the celebration of this mystery as a single lived experience, central to Christian faith and identity. It is not just the commemoration of the last in a series of chronological events from the past.

During Lent, the community was drawn into Christ's way to life through death. During Easter, the focus shifts to the consequences of his risen life in which the baptized already share. Christians already experience Christ's triumph. Its full consequences unfold throughout this season. Through the eucharist, the ongoing sacrament of initiation, believers continually grow into the mystery which Easter celebrates.

## *Mystagogy and the Easter Season*

The term "mystagogy" serves well to describe the ongoing process of becoming Easter people. It designates the church's ancient way of continuing the process of initiation with newly baptized adults (neophytes or newborn) during the fifty days of Easter. The ongoing study of the mysteries which the word implies invites all of us to reflect on the rites, symbols and experiences of the celebrations and to ponder the consequences of initiation for the future. For this reflection to be truly fruitful, full, rich sacramental actions that use lots of water and oil, real bread and a shared cup will be indispensable aspects of each celebration. Strengthened and sustained by the eucharist, the neophytes and the rest of the community ask, "Where do we go from here?" The sacred mystery—the Christian's sacramental immersion into the reality of Christ's death and resurrection—simply cannot be grasped once and for all.

A mystery, in this technical-liturgical-sacramental sense, is not simply a puzzle that cannot be solved, a question that cannot be answered, or an issue that cannot be understood. Rather, it is an open-ended experience so profound and rich that no description or analysis can exhaust its content or meaning. Human love and friendship are good examples of such a mystery: like diamonds with many facets, no amount of analysis or description will adequately express their content.

## *Probing the Mystery*

Throughout the entire season, the church never tires of rejoicing in hope. No more fasting; no more penitential psalms; and, in earlier centuries, no more kneeling: Christ has won his victory and stands in triumph and we, his body, stand with him. Christ, now risen from the dead, cannot die again. Death has no power over him. The ongoing pattern of the church's celebration follows that of the apostles' experience in the resurrection narratives. His story continues to unfold; we continue to discern his presence in word and sacrament.

The first key aspect of this mystery is the person of Christ himself. What is so special about this person that believers have come to experience him as so absolutely unique? What did he live for? What did he die for? The Easter Season invites the community of faith to probe this mystery anew.

The second aspect of the mystery involves the sacraments of Christian initiation celebrated at the Easter vigil after the intense period of Lenten preparation. What does it mean to have been immersed into the death and resurrection of Christ? What does it mean to eat and drink at the Lord's great feast? What will the ongoing consequences of this identity with Christ mean for successive years, generations, even centuries? What does it mean to be a Christian today? Clearly these questions need ongoing exploration. It is thus particularly appropriate that the church, reborn in the sacraments of initiation, celebrate the confirmation and first sharing in holy communion of children and young people on the Sundays of the Easter Season. When Christian initiation happens in persons and families, the season's core meaning comes alive.

The third aspect of the mystery highlights the church, the corporate incarnation of the risen Christ in the unfolding history of the world. The Acts of the Apostles continues to be written throughout the history of the church. We continue to ponder such mysteries as: What does it mean to be church today? How do we best organize ourselves to be effective instruments for living out and communicating the Spirit in which Christ lived, died, and rose?

## *The Mystery Unfolded in the Lectionary*

Throughout the Easter Season, the scripture passages used in the liturgy provide a context for reflecting on the various aspects of the mystery of Christ's rising from the dead. Selections from the Acts of the Apostles dealing with the Spirit-driven work of the risen Christ in the church replace the Old Testament readings throughout the Easter season.

Each of the seven Sundays of Easter unfolds aspects of this mystery in a way that leads to the feast of Pentecost (please see the chart on page 20).

## *The Mystery Unfolded in Symbol*

Integral to this full and rich mystagogical approach are the symbols and elements of the Easter season. The Easter candle stands as a proud herald that darkness has been overcome; it should have pride of place throughout the season. The sprinkling rite, in which we use a fresh springtime branch and ample amounts of fresh water, evokes our baptism during the entrance rite throughout the season. Standing throughout the eucharistic prayer (mandated for the whole of the Easter feast at the Council of Nicea in 325) signals our dignity and solidarity with the "risen one." Other elements—Easter banners, hangings and fresh spring flowers, a gospel procession accompanied by festive alleluias and the use of incense—can contribute greatly to maintaining a festive spirit, as does the consistent use of specifically Easter music throughout the fifty days. All of these reveal aspects of the mystery of the risen Lord, and nourish the community's reflection.

| Sunday | Scripture Yr. A | Scripture Yr. B | Scripture Yr. C | Images and Aspects of the Paschal Mystery; invitations to dying and rising |
|---|---|---|---|---|
| Second Sunday of Easter | John 20: 19-31 A week later, Jesus came and stood among them … | John 20: 19-31 A week later, Jesus came and stood among them … | John 20: 19-31 A week later, Jesus came and stood among them … | Christ's offer of peace; potential for forgiveness and reconciliation in the Spirit; overcoming doubt by being in touch with Christ's woundedness. You have not seen, yet believe. |
| Third Sunday of Easter | Luke 24:13-15 The disciples recognized the Lord when he broke bread with them. | Luke 24:35-48 Thus it is written, that the Messiah is to suffer and to rise from the dead on the third day. | John 21:1-19 Jesus took the bread and gave it to them, and did the same with the fish. | Burning hearts on the road; Jesus discovered in the break-ing of bread; shared food: bread and fish provided by the Risen One; Message of for-giveness to be shared; waiting to be clothed with power from on high; Eucharist: ongoing initiation. |
| Fourth Sunday of Easter | John 10:1-10 I am the gate for the sheep | John 10:11-18 The good shepherd lays down his life for the sheep | John 10:27-30 I give my sheep eternal life. | Christian initiation (Psalm 23); water, oil, feast, overflowing cup; gate to fullness of life; lay down life for others. |
| Fifth Sunday of Easter | John 14:1-12 I am the way, and the truth and the life. | John 15:1-8 Those who abide in me and I in them, bear much fruit | John 13:1, 31-33a, 34-35 I give you a new commandment, that you love one another | Abiding in love; Vine and branches—holy communion; Love as command—a kind of death to self. |
| Sixth Sunday of Easter | John 14:15-21 I will ask the Father and he will give you another advocate | John 15:9-17 No one has greater love than this, to lay down one's life for friends. | John 14:23-29 The Holy Spirit will teach you every-thing and remind you of all that I have said to you | A teaching spirit, An advocate—a lawyer—who is on your side, working in your inner conscience. The joy of Jesus coming alive. Being friends of Jesus |
| Ascension | Matthew 28:16-20 All authority in heaven and earth has been given to me | Mark 16:15-20 The Lord Jesus was taken up into heaven and sat down at the right hand of God | Luke 24:46-53 Jesus withdrew from them and was carried up into heaven | Exaltation of Jesus: new way of being present as the sender of the Spirit from "right hand" of God. Spirit promised in midst of the disciples trembling in doubt; Don't just stand there looking up to heaven. |
| Seventh Sunday of Easter | John 17: 1-11a Jesus looked up to the Father and said, Glorify your son. | John 17:11b-19 May they be one as we are one. | John 17:20-26 Father, may they all be one. | Glorification of God by fini-shing the work of Christ. Christ as ongoing protector. Holiness= sanctification in truth. Sent to the world. Being one. |
| Vigil of Pentecost | John 7:37-39 Out of Jesus' heart shall flow rivers of living water | John 7:37-39 Out of Jesus' heart shall flow rivers of living water | John 7:37-39 Out of Jesus' heart shall flow rivers of living water | The heart of Jesus; Living water, of refreshment and purification. The sacramental life of the church. |
| Pentecost | John 20:19-23 As the Father has sent me, so I send you. | John 15:26-27; 16-12-15 The Spirit of truth will guide you into all the truth. | John 19:15-16;23b-26 The Holy Spirit whom the Father will send in my name will teach you everything. | Holy Spirit as the living presence of Jesus in the believing assembly; "divine indwelling"; being sent: mission to all times, places, cultures to share Spirit. |

## The Mystery Unfolded in the Church

The elements of mystagogy, described earlier—ongoing rejoicing in hope, concern for Christian conduct, and the ongoing ministry of the church—make the Easter season an ideal time to celebrate the various ministries in the community and to imagine new and more creative ways to serve in the Spirit of the risen Christ.

It is appropriate to present pastoral council and other reports, and even hold elections at this time. Celebrating ministry, and encouraging and facilitating ongoing renewal in ministry affirm and challenge the community to continue to manifest the risen Christ (the body of Christ) in the world.

The whole parish needs to see how this period of mystagogy embraces all: how the local gathering of faithful experiences its baptismal energy; how this assembly deals with obstacles to its effective mission to the world. It needs to identify the Spirit's ongoing invitations here and now, the signs of hope and promise at work in the community and the world, and learn how to foster and encourage them. It is a time for the parish to discover how to discern the presence of the risen Christ in every aspect of this experience of faith, hope and love. The neophytes' presence in the community is the clearest sign of the church's ongoing renewal and rejuvenation; their presence is fully effective only when it touches the life of the whole community and invites it to take a fresh look at the world in the light of the gospel. Children and young people celebrating first eucharist and confirmation, together with their families and friends, join the newly baptized as a sign of hope and promise for the community.

The living experience of these people, linked with the whole community's springtime, paschal renewal gives impetus and direction to the whole season. In this context, the fifty-day feast actually begins to feel too short!

## Springtime and the Easter Season

The chapter on Lent refers to its springtime roots and to the cosmic proportions of the paschal mystery. The second reading of

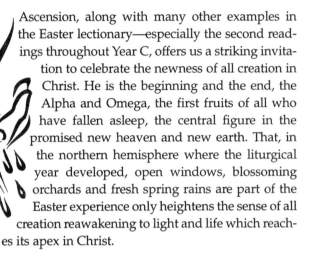

Ascension, along with many other examples in the Easter lectionary—especially the second readings throughout Year C, offers us a striking invitation to celebrate the newness of all creation in Christ. He is the beginning and the end, the Alpha and Omega, the first fruits of all who have fallen asleep, the central figure in the promised new heaven and new earth. That, in the northern hemisphere where the liturgical year developed, open windows, blossoming orchards and fresh spring rains are part of the Easter experience only heightens the sense of all creation reawakening to light and life which reaches its apex in Christ.

## Sticky Issues

During liturgical preparation, questions about Mother's Day and May as a month of popular devotion to Mary can sometimes be a source of contention. Although not directly or specifically related to the Easter Season, the values and traditions behind these observances deserve respect and consideration, especially in communities with strong ethnic backgrounds. Using a little imagination, a homilist can relate such biblical images of the season as abiding in love, the vine and the branches, and the good shepherd to the unique vocation of parents. The role of Mary, who stood with other women and John at the foot of the cross and found her place with the disciples after the resurrection (as the Pentecost story makes clear) can find its place in preaching, prayers and hymns throughout the season. The *Magnificat* (Mary's song in Luke 1), a permanent feature of evening prayer, provides an excellent example of mystagogy. Mary ponders what she has just experienced and proclaims the significance of her call to bear Christ to the world. Only in light of the resurrection can the full meaning of this experience be discovered. Such considerations cannot be allowed to dominate the liturgy, but can be quite effectively integrated into it as part of the paschal tapestry.

## Celebrating Evening Prayer During the Season

Liturgy teams can prepare forms of morning and evening prayer based on the liturgy of hours for homes, schools and occasions such as parish meetings (*Catholic Book of Worship III* offers a fine model). Even if the attendance is small, parishes can celebrate evening prayer on Sundays throughout the season. Various members of the community can be prepared to preside. The celebration includes a procession with the paschal candle, a thanksgiving for the light that echoes the *Exsultet* of the Easter Vigil, a traditional Easter hymn, appropriate psalms, a scripture reading (perhaps the second reading from the Sunday), a brief homily if so desired, the *Magnificat*, intercessory prayer, the Lord's prayer and the exchange of peace. This prayer can be a beautiful experience on the Sunday evenings of Easter. Experience shows that this kind of celebration can slowly develop as an integral part of a community's celebration of Easter.

## Catechesis

Mystagogy is the church's great tradition of catechesis appropriate to this season. The mystagogical catechesis of early church leaders centres on the meaning and consequences of baptism and eucharist for life in this world, and as foretaste and promise of the world to come. While the church rejoices, bathed in the light of the risen Christ, scriptural texts and prayers of the season focus on Christian conduct and mission to the world in communion with Christ. Out of Easter joy comes a determination to live the Christian life to the full and to share it with others in the spirit of Jesus who said: "My Father is glorified by this, that you bear much fruit and become my disciples. As the Father has loved me, so I have loved you; abide in my love. If you keep my commandments, you will abide in my love, just as I have kept my Father's commandments and abide in his love. I have said these things to you so that my joy may be in you, and that your joy may be complete" (John 15:8-11, Easter VI-B).

Rejoicing, renewed insight into the consequences of the resurrection for Christian conduct, and a heightened sense of mission suggest the fundamental attitudes of Easter life—a grateful response to what God has done for believers in the resurrection of Jesus. They constitute the core catechetical content of Easter.

## *Priorities*

Those preparing the fifty-day Easter liturgy will need to remind themselves over and over again to look at the season as a unified feast. This is not an easy assignment in a cultural context which tends to celebrate one-day feasts such as Canada Day, or a feast such as Christmas, which has a drawn out, sometimes frenetic preparatory period and screeches prematurely to an abrupt end.

Focusing on solidarity with persons being initiated, on the experience of springtime as an unfolding season, and on the need for renewal and rejuvenation in the community's sense of purposeful, Spirit-filled ministry will gradually forge the sense of the fifty days as a single, integrated event.

## *In Summary*

1. During Easter, the Christian community celebrates the paschal mystery in the liberty and victory which is already ours through sharing in Christ's death and rising. Christ's triumph promises our own.

2. Thus, the Easter season joyfully anticipates the victory that already belongs in hope to those who share faith in Christ's risen life.

3. Through the entire season of fifty days, the community never tires of rejoicing in hope. The triumphant alleluia is proclaimed incessantly. There are no penitential psalms, no fasting, no kneeling, only confident, festive rejoicing in paschal light.

## Discussion Questions

1. How can we make sure that alienated Catholics, the house-bound or disabled persons who join us just during the Easter season—on Easter Sunday, and for celebrations such as first communion and confirmation—feel welcome? How might we invite them to return at other times?

2. Does our celebration of Easter last fifty days or does it fizzle out after the Second Sunday of Easter? What would help us sustain it the full fifty days? You might want to consider music, environment, homilies.

3. Does our celebration of the Easter season feel different from Ordinary Time?

4. Do we schedule the celebration of initiation sacraments—first communion and confirmation—during the Easter Season and help people understand the link between the event and the season?

5. Are our symbols and rituals strong and festive enough to provide a foundation for mystagogy? Have we allowed the special gestures and symbols of the season to stand out? Can the assembly associate the sprinkling rite, the paschal candle in a special way with Easter? How might we enhance this appreciation?

6. As a finale to the great fifty days, does our celebration of Pentecost affirm the giftedness of the whole church and the diversity of gifts the community shares? How can we enhance or sustain this celebration?

7. How do we incorporate the coming of springtime and the revival of the natural world with the liturgical life and spirituality of this community?

8. What role does the liturgy of hours play during the Lent-Easter season? What role could it play?

# CHAPTER 3

# The Advent-Christmas Season

In a way which has its own unique colour and flavour, the celebration of the Sundays and feasts of the Advent-Christmas season centres, as does all Christian liturgy, on the paschal mystery. In the northern hemisphere, preparation for the feast of Christmas takes place in a time of growing darkness. The season of Advent, which means "coming," announces to a world where darkness overtakes light each day that our personal lives, and even the life of the world as we know it, will come to an end. Wondrously, the comings of Christ transcend space and time and call believers to joyful hope as they anticipate his coming in glory. Conscious that it lives between Christ's appearance in the flesh and the full flowering of his cosmic presence in the end-time, the church lives and prays in hope, trusting in his promise to "be with you always, even to the end of time" (Matthew 28:20).

As the light of the autumn sun wanes and each day grows shorter, faith rests in the assurance that night will never last forever. Like the lengthening days that will slowly announce spring's dawning, the light of Christ will finally rise upon the world's darkness.

The season begins with the awesome consideration of final judgment. It sounds the note of serious anticipation of the Lord who expects believers to have their houses in order, and proclaims the confidence derived from knowing that the judge is a loving Saviour of flesh and blood—"one of us in all things but sin" (Hebrews 4:15).

## The Challenges of Advent

In Advent, a whole spectrum of figures whose common element is hope confronts the Christian community. Ancient Israel's hope for home, security and a peaceful world will be rooted in the person and activity of the Messiah. The figure of John the Baptist stands between civilization and the desert, dressed in camel's hair, as a dramatic and radical challenge to all that is comfortable and secure. His summons to wake up to conversion and renewal is a sign of hope to his listeners that there really can be a better world. Jesus' words and Paul's early epistles take to new heights ancient messianic expectations and prophetic calls to conversion. The whole world as we know it is passing away: with this in mind, the season challenges believers to evaluate and judge their personal, social and cultural lives and experience. The perspective of God's final judgment and the reality of the life of the world to come invite us to a deeper and more committed way of being human today. God's promise and fidelity provide the foundation for the universal goal of peace and communion that give us light and courage in the inevitable tensions of an "in-between" lifestyle.

Such considerations strike a strong, almost modern, note. In our contemporary world, we cannot take faith for granted. Evil in the world, personal failure, sickness, tragedy, human stupidity and institutional corruption threaten people's confidence in the goodness of life and the reality of God's love. In times of rapid transition and social, economic and cultural instability, the sense of being overwhelmed and powerless tempts even those who think their faith is strong.

## *Hope*

Advent's hope speaks to this void in poetic, even mystical ways. Israel's prophecies of hope were delivered to a people who were experiencing darkness, defeat and exile. John the Baptist discovered God's ways in the isolation and desolation of the wilderness. Mary gives birth to the Saviour of the world in poverty and obscurity. Believers are invited to grasp the ancient paradox that God is often most present and active when he seems absent and inactive.

With a kind of hindsight, the community savours these ancient stories and images. It sees the prophecies of the Hebrew scriptures fulfilled in Christ's coming and in his continued unseen presence which will one day be fully revealed. The figure of John the Baptist receives special prominence as he calls the community to attention and challenges the values and standards of the world. The call to "prepare the way of the Lord and to make straight his path" goes out to every age. The Virgin Mary, herself one of the poor and lowly, is pregnant with the word of God. She stands as a sign and invitation to faithful, watchful, creative waiting and openness to life.

All of this resounds with clear paschal connotations. A careful look at such realities as racism, military build-ups, the growing gap between rich and poor, the pollution of the environment, etc. in light of the scriptures appointed for proclamation during the Advent-Christmas season will lead us to yet another experience of dying and rising. Any of Isaiah's texts will invite us to rethink and reorder our priorities.

## *The Mystery Unfolded in the Lectionary*

While there is a danger inherent in looking for clear "themes" in the lectionary, those responsible for preparing liturgical celebrations will want to know it well. Look at each season as a whole, and try to understand the particular perspective that each of the years of the three-year cycle brings.

The theme of every Christian celebration is the paschal mystery. The various configurations of biblical texts enable the believing assembly to consider and celebrate the mystery of dying and rising from many different points of view, which, with their varying colours and textures, make the experience of the season a kind of tapestry. The following table of gospels for the Advent-Christmas season, with the accompanying headings taken from the lectionary and suggestions for the aspect of the paschal mystery being proclaimed, provide a good starting point for preparing the season from this perspective. The aspects suggested are just examples of the ways in which the paschal mystery can be viewed through the lenses of individual texts.

For fuller details and complete charts, see Adrien Nocent,
O.S.B., *The Liturgical Year*, four volumes, (Collegeville: The
Liturgical Press, 1977) and Normand Bonneau, *The Sunday
Lectionary: Ritual Word, Paschal Shape*, (Collegeville: The
Liturgical Press, 1998).

| Sunday | Scripture Yr. A | Scripture Yr. B | Scripture Yr. C | Images and Aspects of the Paschal Mystery; invitations to dying and rising |
|---|---|---|---|---|
| First Sunday of Advent | Matthew 24:37- Keep awake, therefore, you also must be ready | Mark 13:31-37 Keep alert, for you do not know when the Lord will come. | Luke 21:25-28; 34-36 Your redemption is drawing near. | Attentiveness; the world as we know it passes; judgment as personal and societal accountability to God; ultimate vindication of the good. |
| Second Sunday of Advent | Matthew 3: 1-12 Repent, for the kingdom of heaven has come near. | Mark 1: 1-8 Prepare the way of the Lord. | Luke 3: 1-6 All flesh shall see the salvation of God. | Figure of the Baptist; readiness for what is new; urgency: no time to waste; openness to change, even dramatic change; repentance, conversion. |
| Third Sunday of Advent | Matthew 11:2-11 Are you the one who is to come, or are we to wait for another? | John 1: 6-8, 19-28 among you stands one whom you do not know, the one who is coming after me | Luke 3: 10-18 The crowds asked, "What should we do?" | Figure of the Baptist; Who is the Christ for me? for us? What does faith demand? |
| Fourth Sunday of Advent | Matthew 1: 18-24 Jesus was born of Mary, who was engaged to Joseph, son of David. | Luke 1:26-38 You will conceive in your womb and bear a son. | Luke 1: 39-45 Why has this happened to me, that the mother of my Lord comes to me? | Figure of Mary; openness to God, to the future; risk, adventure; saying "amen," let it be. |

## Christmas and the Paschal Mystery

The incarnation, in which God takes on human flesh and is
born into time and space, engages a mysterious kind of death:
At the very heart of God a kind of "death to self" is happening.
The famous text from Philippians 2:6-11, read on Palm Sunday,
shows the fundamental unity of the Christmas and Easter mysteries. Both invite us to participate in Christ's dying and rising—a process which begins in the incarnation.

The biblical conviction that humans are created in the image and likeness of God is powerfully re-expressed in the person of Jesus, Emmanuel, God-with-us. That "same mind" is to be in all who believe. In Jesus, the true potential of humanity and the true dignity of all of creation are revealed.

In their homilies during this season, ancient church teachers referred to a wonderful exchange: God shares human nature so that humans might share more fully in the divine. The opening prayer of the Mass of Christmas Day expresses this same faith:

> *Lord, God, we praise you for creating our human family*
> *and still more for restoring us in Christ.*
> *Your Son shared our weakness:*
> *may we share his glory ...*

## The Core of the Christmas Season

The core celebration of the Christmas season is made up of three great feasts: Christmas, Epiphany, and the Baptism of the Lord. It also embraces Holy Family (the Sunday after Christmas), Mary, Mother of God (January 1, the Octave of Christmas), the Second Sunday of Christmas and three feasts which follow immediately after Christmas Day: Saint Stephen, the first martyr on December 26, Saint John, apostle and evangelist on December 27, and Holy Innocents on December 28.

Although they seem separate, careful reflection reveals that each feast points to and celebrates an aspect of the paschal mystery. The gospels for the three feasts which follow immediately on the heels of Christmas are particularly noteworthy. If viewed from outside the perspective of the paschal mystery, they seem more typical of the Easter than the Christmas season.

## The Mystery Unfolded in the Lectionary

Note that the directive in the lectionary indicates that the readings from any of the Christmas masses may be used according to pastoral needs, i.e., night, dawn and day texts are not restricted to use exclusively at that particular time.

Noteworthy as well is the repetition of the prologue from John's gospel from the Mass of Christmas Day on the Second Sunday after Christmas. In the second instance, it is accompanied, not by Isaiah 52:7-10, which deals with the beauty of the messenger bringing peace, but by Sirach 24:1-4, 8-12, which presents the eternal wisdom in all her glory making a tent on the earth. In Christ are made incarnate this eternal word and eternal wisdom. Every aspect of the wonder and mystery of God is manifested in the flesh.

| Sunday | Scripture Yr. A | Scripture Yr. B | Scripture Yr. C | Images and Aspects of the Paschal Mystery; invitations to dying and rising |
|---|---|---|---|---|
| Vigil of Christmas | Matthew 1: 1-25 An account of the genealogy of Jesus, the Messiah, Son of David | Matthew 1: 1-25 An account of the genealogy of Jesus, the Messiah, Son of David | Matthew 1: 1-25 An account of the genealogy of Jesus, the Messiah, Son of David | Rootedness in human history; surprising new beginning; Joseph the dreamer; risky trust in dream. |
| Christmas: Mass During the Night | Luke 2: 1-16 To you is born this day a Saviour, who is the Messiah | Luke 2: 1-16 To you is born this day a Saviour, who is the Messiah | Luke 2: 1-16 To you is born this day a Saviour, who is the Messiah | A new beginning in the midst of darkness and poverty; Do not be afraid—good news! The glory of God in peace on earth. |
| Mass at Dawn | Luke 2: 15-20 The shepherds found Mary and Joseph, and the child lying in the manger | Luke 2: 15-20 The shepherds found Mary and Joseph, and the child lying in the manger | Luke 2: 15-20 The shepherds found Mary and Joseph, and the child lying in the manger | Seeking and finding; going back praising; treasuring and pondering |
| Mass During the Day | John 1:1-18 The Word became flesh and lived among us, and we have seen his glory. | John 1:1-18 The Word became flesh and lived among us, and we have seen his glory. | John 1:1-18 The Word became flesh and lived among us, and we have seen his glory. | Eternal Word made flesh; Pre-existent Word: universal Cosmic Christ stretches boundaries of faith; From his fullness we all have received—grace upon grace. |
| Holy Family | Matthew 2: 13-15, 19-23. Get up, take the child and his mother, and flee to Egypt | Luke 2: 22-40 The child grew, filled with wisdom, and the favour of God was upon him. | Luke 2: 41-52 His parents found him in the temple, sitting among the teachers, and they were astonished. | Human experience of Christ—growing; Family: focus on community, rootedness over against individualism. |

| Mary, Mother of God | Luke 2:16-21 The shepherds found Mary and Joseph and the child lying in the manger. After eight days he was named Jesus. | Luke 2:16-21 The shepherds found Mary and Joseph and the child lying in the manger. After eight days he was named Jesus. | Luke 2:16-21 The shepherds found Mary and Joseph and the child lying in the manger. After eight days he was named Jesus. | Mary as model disciple: treasuring and pondering. "Mothering the Christ" in our own time: Mary as model of the church's mission. |
|---|---|---|---|---|
| Second Sunday after Christmas | John 1: 1-18 The Word became flesh and lived among us and we have seen his glory | John 1: 1-18 The Word became flesh and lived among us and we have seen his glory | John 1: 1-18 The Word became flesh and lived among us and we have seen his glory | Unfolding mystery of the incarnation. See also Christmas Day. |
| Epiphany | Matthew 2: 1-12 We have come from the east to pay homage to the king. | Matthew 2: 1-12 We have come from the east to pay homage to the king. | Matthew 2: 1-12 We have come from the east to pay homage to the king. | Following a star by the wise; universalism. |
| Baptism of Our Lord | Matthew 3; 13-17 When Jesus had been baptized, he saw the Spirit of God coming upon him. | Mark 1: 7-11 You are my son, the beloved; with you I am well pleased. | Luke 3:15-16, 21-22 When Jesus had been baptized and was praying, the heaven was opened, and the Holy Spirit descended upon him. | Call-vocation; New beginnings-new Israel Baptism as enlightenment. |

# Christmas

The celebration of Jesus' birth on December 25 roughly corresponds with the winter solstice, when the sun appears to rise in its orbit and long winter nights begin to grow shorter. For the ancients, this was a major time of festivity as the return of the light brought promise of springtime renewal. In its own way, the church takes over this festival as it sees and acknowledges Christ as the rising "sun of righteousness with healing in its rays" (Malachi 4:2).

While the earliest generations of the church did not celebrate this feast, they did make extensive use of the biblical image of light to describe Christ's coming and Christ's reign. The figure of Christ, light of the world and splendour of the Father's glory, receives special attention and takes on universal, even cosmic, proportions in the liturgical celebrations of the whole season.

## Epiphany

The prologue of John's gospel, which is key to the celebration of Christmas, proclaims Christ as the eternal Word through whom all things were made, the life of the world, the light that can never be conquered, the one who endures as grace upon grace for all who accept him. In the celebration of Christ's coming, the glory of God is first revealed in the humility of a baby whose shelter is a stable and whose presence is made known only to a few rough, simple shepherds. The circle of those who discover God in him grows. At Epiphany we see that the invitation which its star offers extends beyond the household of Israel to men and women of every time and place.

## The Baptism of the Lord

The Baptism of the Lord presents a heavenly voice proclaiming him the Beloved Son, ongoing source of illumination and renewal. His final coming may well be far off, but the work of redemption has begun. The seeds of the divine sharing have been planted so that humans might share the divine. Heaven joins with earth so that earth may join with heaven. In the mystery of baptism, believers experience their communion with this child of humanity against whom sin is powerless. His flesh and blood shared in eucharist are already a sharing in his new world.

The season celebrates living faith more than historical events. That is why we proclaim in the Nicene Creed and genuflect this season as we do so:

> *We believe in one Lord, Jesus Christ,*
> *the only Son of God,*
> *eternally begotten of the Father,*
> *God from God, Light from Light,*
> *true God from true God,*
> *begotten, not made, one in Being with the Father.*
> *Through him all things were made.*
> *For us men and for our salvation*
> *he came down from heaven:*
> *by the power of the Holy Spirit*
> *he was born of the Virgin Mary, and became man.*

## *Working with the Spirit of the Season*

The spirit of the season, even with its excesses, can express the joy and wonder of this profound truth. Greetings, best wishes and gifts affirm the goodness and wonder of human family and friendship. Lights and flowers drive away darkness and winter. People welcome guests into their homes. Our consciousness of the presence of the poor is heightened and we redouble our efforts on their behalf. People gather around the shining tree of life as they proclaim and celebrate the possibility of new beginnings as a new calendar year begins.

Keeping Christmas, Christ's festival—even with the "excessive merriment" roundly criticized at certain points of Christian history, stands as a witness to hope, to human dignity and potential, and to the cosmic character of Christ's ongoing grace and influence.

This season can powerfully express the church's overall mission to be a sign and herald of an eternal feast that embraces all people and characterizes the reign of God. At Epiphany, people mysterious and wise gather to celebrate Christ's manifestation to the nations with a new star in the heavens. At Jesus' baptism, a heavenly voice proclaims him "beloved." A Spirit hovers over the waters as at the very beginning of time: here is a new creation, a new source of unity for all humanity.

The central challenge for those responsible for preparing the liturgy during this season will be to facilitate the assembly's participation in these aspects of the mystery of God's love. Because of the hectic pace of the season, and the high expectations of family, friends and community, planners will need to emphasize Christ's coming in the flesh and the community's ongoing waiting in hope (incarnation and eschatology). That God becomes part of the reality of human life with all its tensions and all its ambivalence and opens a path to healing, reconciliation and communion is a life-giving aspect of the paschal mystery, especially for broken persons and families who experience the "Christmas spirit" as a kind of judgment. Celebrating the sacrament of reconciliation during this season can slow us down so we can invite the "sun of justice" with "healing in its wings" to be present and active with "mercy mild" for "peace on earth."

## The Figure of Mary

In this context, the figure of Mary is particularly powerful. Her yes to the angel's invitation, her pregnancy, her song of justice and the transformation of the world that she sings when meeting Elizabeth, her journey to the city of her people's roots to give birth to a whole new era of human history, her reception of shepherds and foreigners, and her treasuring of all this in her heart highlight her prophetic role in the paschal mystery which will unfold in the life of her son.

## Pageants, Parties and the Liturgy

Very concrete and practical considerations will arise: carol festivals, children's pageants, Christmas parties, etc. and their relationship to the liturgical celebrations. All of these have an important place in the overall experience of Christmas, even in the secular culture. Communities need to embrace them and situate these activities in the overall experience of the season without letting them take over the main thrust of the liturgy.

Apart from the principal liturgies, a special evening for parents and children, with song, dance, pageants and tableaux can be wonderful fun. Lighting Advent wreaths and Christmas trees, although secondary in the liturgy, can be prominent in home, school, and extra-liturgical church celebrations. Those responsible for liturgical preparation should be pro-active in suggesting and providing resources, and hosting such opportunities rather than simply being negative about including them in the liturgy.

During this season, the presence of many visitors and "once or twice a year Catholics" at liturgies presents its own challenge. Using traditional music that invites and includes these persons and the tone and content of welcoming remarks and the homily will go a long way towards expressing the true Christmas spirit of outreach and inclusion.

## Traditions of the Season

Those preparing the liturgy will also need to consider how to use and incorporate into the liturgy secondary elements, such as the Advent wreath, which have become traditions of the season.

### The Advent Wreath

The focus on the passage from darkness to light, the fidelity of evergreen branches, and the circle, sign of God's own eternal, inclusive embrace is certainly in keeping with the overall paschal content of the season. These elements can best be included in the liturgy's opening rites, which set the tone of the celebration, but they are most effective elsewhere, for example, as the centrepiece of a family's table prayer.

*Sunday Celebrations of the Word and Hours* (Ottawa: Canadian Conference of Catholic Bishops, 1995, p. 4) provides a lovely prayer of praise over the Advent wreath.

### The Crèche

The crèche is another example of a very popular, traditional secondary symbol. Although a procession with the statue of the baby Jesus and elaborate blessing rites should be discouraged as they distract from the main emphasis of the liturgy, the crèche is still an important part of the environment in most churches. Ideally it will have a place all its own, away from the altar, where children can get close enough to really appreciate and enjoy it, or others can pause to contemplate. Look around for a suitable place: an alcove, a side chapel, or a site near the entrance to the church. To place it under the altar or in any other central position in the sanctuary both de-emphasizes the altar as table and makes the crèche itself less accessible.

## *Music*

Music is another element in Christmas festivity which needs special attention. It has been said that if ever the assembly is going to be really singing, it is at Christmas with its familiar hymns and carols. Many of these texts have an explicitly "paschal flavor" which can be very useful in preaching and catechesis.

One of the challenges of the Christmas season is finding suitable music to sing through to the feast of the Baptism of the Lord, when "O Come, All Ye Faithful" just does not seem—and is not—appropriate. The major images of the season provide additional guidance for your choice. Read through your hymn book carefully; you may find other very suitable texts and tunes outside the Christmas section.

The following text is given because it illustrates well a liturgical text that has been designed specifically for use during the Christmas season, and set to a familiar carol tune. Set to the tune better known as "Once in Royal David's City," it was designed as a processional (see #346 in *Catholic Book of Worship III*).

## In The Darkness Shines The Splendour

1.

*In the darkness shines the splendour*
*Of the Word who took our flesh,*
*Welcoming, in love's surrender,*
*Death's dark shadow at his crèche.*
*Bearing ev'ry human story,*
*Word made flesh reveals his glory.*

2.

*Light of nations, veiled in hist'ry,*
*Born of woman's flesh and blood,*
*Calling to the depths of myst'ry*
*Restless hearts that seek the good.*
*Healing ev'ry human story,*
*Word made flesh reveals his glory.*

3.

*Broken bread, sustaining us in sorrow,*
*Wine poured out to toast our joy;*
*Exodus and new tomorrow,*
*Life's full promise to enjoy!*
*Gladd'ning ev'ry human story,*
*Word made flesh reveals his glory.*

4.

*All God's people, sing in jubilation*
*Of the birth that sets us free,*
*Telling of the revelation:*
*Jesus, God's epiphany.*
*Celebrate the human story!*
*Word made flesh reveals our glory.*

Copyright © 1992, Bernadette Gasslein, 1952-
Tune: IRBY

## *Catechesis*

The key element in the Advent-Christmas season is the experience of the manifold coming and manifestation of God in Christ. This experience invites the whole world to renewal. Woven together in a glorious tapestry are the coming of Christ in the flesh, the movement of God in Christ to embrace all humanity, and Christ's promise to come in fullness and glory on the last day to draw all creation to reconciliation and peace. Catechesis and preaching during this season will invite the assembly to move beyond the birth of Jesus at Bethlehem into this broader experience.

## *Priorities*

As in all things liturgical, the priorities will be paschal. Because of the almost overpowering influence of culture on the experience of Christmas, the liturgy will seek to enable people to participate in and commune with the central mystery of faith. It will strive for serenity and depth rather than competing with the culture for attention.

## *In Summary*

The following hymn text summarizes the paschal mystery's flavour during the Advent-Christmas season. It represents the Christmas way of proclaiming that "Christ has died; Christ is risen; Christ will come again."

1.

*Of the Father's love begotten,*
*Ere the worlds began to be,*
*He is Alpha and Omega,*
*He the source, the ending he,*
*Of the things that are, that have been,*
*And that future years shall see,*
*Evermore and evermore!*

2.

*O that birth for ever blessed*
*When the Virgin, full of grace,*
*By the Spirit blest conceiving,*
*Bore the Saviour of our race;*
*And the babe, the world's Redeemer,*
*First revealed his sacred face,*
*Evermore and evermore!*

3.

*Let the heights of heav'n adore him;*
*Angel hosts, his praises sing;*
*Pow'rs, dominions, bow before him,*
*And extol our God and King;*
*Let no tongue on earth be silent,*
*Ev'ry voice in concert ring,*
*Evermore and evermore!*

4.

*Christ, to you with God the Father,*
*Spirit blest, eternally,*
*Hymn and chant and high thanksgiving,*
*And unending praises be:*
*Honour, glory and dominion,*
*And eternal victory,*
*Evermore and evermore!*

Text: Corde natus ex parentis; Aurelius Prudentius, 348-413. Translation: John Mason Neale, 1818-1866 and Henry Williams Baker, 1821-1877; alt.

## Discussion Questions

1. How is the second coming understood in our community? How can this season enhance our appreciation of the final destiny of all of creation.

2. Do we really believe in the incarnation? Do we believe in and experience God in the stuff of creation—people, bread, wine, water, oil, time, darkness, light, touch, smell, etc.? How do our liturgical celebrations invite a deeper realization and experience of this Christmas truth?

3. Do we experience a Christmas season other than the one proposed by the culture (mid-October to December 24)? How can we hold and sustain the season through to the feast of the Baptism of Our Lord?

# A Timeless Event Celebrated in Time

In the introduction to volume 1, I alluded to psalm 90 as recast in "O God, Our Help in Ages Past." The hymn speaks of "time like an ever-rolling stream" which "bears all our lives away." This view of time proceeds relentlessly forward, with no possibility of turning back.

We contrasted this view of time with liturgical time which, in the Christian tradition, centres on a particular "timeless" event: the death and resurrection of Christ. This moment is so central to human history and so dense with meaning that all of humanity is invited to enter into it. Jesus' passover from death to life becomes a contemporary reality for all who respond to the invitation to be drawn into communion with it.

The scriptures indicate that the heavens and earth are shaken and the sun darkened when Christ dies, that a huge stone is suddenly rolled back when he rises, and that a new star appears in the sky when he was born. Jesus, the Christ is an event of cosmic proportions. For those who believe, all time and space are permeated with his ongoing presence. In word and sacrament, Christ's death and rising are truly present for believers, drawing them into this experience so they can see it as the foundation for interpreting the meaning of their own lives.

The liturgy proclaims and celebrates this timelessness. Of the many liturgical texts which affirm and describe it, the Easter proclamation, the *Exsultet*, sung in the light of the paschal candle is perhaps the most powerful example. Notice the present tense throughout:

*This is the passover feast, when Christ, the true lamb is slain, whose blood consecrates the homes of all believers.*

*This is the night when Christians everywhere, washed clean of sin and freed from all defilement, are restored to grace and grow together in holiness.*

*This is the night when Jesus Christ broke the chains of death and rose triumphant from the grave.*

This kind of language announces clearly that time is not simply passing. The memory of this "past event" is unlike any other.

This language does not repeat the past, nor does it return to the past through the mind or imagination. No. In the mystery of word and sacrament, the event is present, touching the believing community and moving it forward. While this kind of memory does recall a past event, it recognizes at the same time its present, living reality and energy, and its promise for the future. The most familiar memorial acclamation of the Eucharistic Prayer summarizes this most succinctly:

"Let us proclaim the mystery of faith. Christ has died; Christ is risen; Christ will come again." This timeless reality encompasses past, present and future—memory, presence and hope.

## Everything Revolves Around This Core

For parish ministers and all who are involved in preparing liturgical celebrations, keeping this foundational experience before their own eyes and hearts provides a core out of which to work. Everything about liturgy must be seen as revolving around this hub and must contribute to its dynamism. The paschal mystery is being made present.

Concretely, this kind of thinking streamlines and simplifies the process of preparation. Working on the liturgical year will help those responsible for preparation, as well as the whole assembly, focus on what is most basic to the Christian life, and help them to experience this same reality from its many varied angles.

They will not develop themes or create liturgical celebrations and experiences. Instead, they will respond to what the liturgical year offers, and prepare the elements of the liturgy in such a way that they support the basic paschal content. Rather than innovate, they will be creative and imaginative with what already exists. Those who have been involved in this ministry for years can testify to how it has deepened their sense of the many splendours of the paschal mystery and developed their biblical-liturgical spirituality that they are ever more eager to share with others.

Another liberating insight gleaned from working with this approach to liturgical preparation (as opposed to planning) is that ministers no longer work from Sunday to Sunday but from year to year. They look at a whole block of ordinary time, for example, choosing elements which will be common to a whole series of Sundays so that the assembly is not surprised or entertained by the liturgy, but invited to participate more deeply. They prepare the whole of the Advent-Christmas section of the year as a unit. They see the Lent-Easter cycle as one. Thus, they can evaluate their experience from year to year, building on what has effectively facilitated the assembly's full, conscious, and active participation in the celebration of the paschal mystery over a more extended period of time. This contributes to building a real sense of tradition.

All in all, what is required is a "stubborn determination" to honour the paschal mystery as the central focus of every celebration, to respect the lead of the lectionary in discovering the aspect of this great mystery to be highlighted during a season or block of Sundays, and to encourage generous use of the symbols—bread, wine, water, light, oil. In this way, ministers genuinely respect people as they invite them to be an assembly sharing fully in the rich and solid food offered at the table of the word and the table of the eucharist, as they invite them to be and to become the Body of Christ.

End Time: Refers to the culmination and completion of life as we know it. The ultimate destiny of all persons of all humanity, and of all creation. Begun and heralded in the death and resurrection of Christ who leads all humanity and all the world into a new creation to be fully revealed at the end of time.

Evening Prayer: A traditional form of Christian prayer, drawn largely from the Bible and celebrated by the community toward the end of day. Often called Vespers.

Mystagogy: The continuing introduction of newly baptized persons into the full, ongoing meaning and consequences of the way of life into which they have been initiated through the sacraments. It involves the incorporation and integration of new members into the fullness of the community's life of worship and service through prayer, teaching, and the experience of the Christian life.

Scrutinies: Literally a testing of persons preparing for baptism. A ritual involving an expression on their part of willingness to live the challenging call of the gospel, and prayers (exorcisms) for the healing of all in them that is weak, defective, or sinful and for the strengthening of all that is upright, strong, and good.

Solstice: Either of the two times of the year when the sun is at its greatest distance from the celestial equator; about June 21, when the sun reaches its northernmost point on the celestial sphere or about December 22 when it reaches its southernmost point. The winter solstice, for example, in the northern hemisphere (December 22) marks the longest night of the year and heralds the beginning of the gradual lengthening of days. Significant in the establishment of seasons and religious feasts related to the cycles of nature.

BIBLIOGRAPHY

## *Recommended Reading*

### Books

Adam, Adolph. *The Liturgical Year: Its History and Meaning After the Reform of the Liturgy*, (N.Y.: Pueblo, 1981). A classic.

Bonneau, Normand, O.M.I. *The Sunday Lectionary: Ritual Word, Paschal Shape*, (Collegeville: Liturgical Press, 1998).

Mick, Lawrence E. *Sourcebook for Sundays and Seasons*, (Chicago: LTP, published annually). Something for every day of the church year.

Nocent, Adrian, O.S.B. *The Liturgical Year*, (Collegeville: Liturgical Press, 1977). Published in six volumes.

Talley, Thomas *The Origins of the Liturgical Year* (N.Y.: Pueblo, 1986). A classic, but hard reading for the uninitiated.

Whalen, Michael D. *Seasons and Feasts of the Church Year* (Mahwah, N.J.: Paulist Press, 1992). An excellent popular introduction.

### Periodicals

*Celebrate!* Novalis, 49 Front Street, 2nd floor, Toronto, Ontario, Canada M5E 1B3. Award-winning Canadian liturgical periodical; topical articles; commentaries for Sundays and feasts.

*liturgical ministry.* Liturgical Press, Saint John's Abbey, Collegeville, Minnesota 56321-7500. Scholarly and pastoral focuses characterize this journal.

*National Bulletin on Liturgy.* Publications Service, Canadian Conference of Catholic Bishops, 90 Parent Avenue, Ottawa, Ontario, Canada K1N 7B1

*Today's Liturgy,* Oregon Catholic Press, 5536 NE Hassalo, Portland, Oregon 97213-3638. Focuses on music ministers.